A Year of Sanctions against Russia—Now What?

A European Assessment of the Outcome and Future of Russia Sanctions

Author
Simond de Galbert

A Report of the CSIS Europe Program

October 2015

CSIS | CENTER FOR STRATEGIC &
INTERNATIONAL STUDIES

ROWMAN *&*
LITTLEFIELD

Lanham • Boulder • New York • London

About CSIS

For over 50 years, the Center for Strategic and International Studies (CSIS) has worked to develop solutions to the world's greatest policy challenges. Today, CSIS scholars are providing strategic insights and bipartisan policy solutions to help decisionmakers chart a course toward a better world.

CSIS is a nonprofit organization headquartered in Washington, D.C. The Center's 220 full-time staff and large network of affiliated scholars conduct research and analysis and develop policy initiatives that look into the future and anticipate change.

Founded at the height of the Cold War by David M. Abshire and Admiral Arleigh Burke, CSIS was dedicated to finding ways to sustain American prominence and prosperity as a force for good in the world. Since 1962, CSIS has become one of the world's preeminent international institutions focused on defense and security; regional stability; and transnational challenges ranging from energy and climate to global health and economic integration.

Former U.S. senator Sam Nunn has chaired the CSIS Board of Trustees since 1999. Former deputy secretary of defense John J. Hamre became the Center's president and chief executive officer in 2000.

CSIS does not take specific policy positions; accordingly, all views expressed herein should be understood to be solely those of the author(s).

ISBN: 978-1-4422-5892-1 (pb); 978-1-4422-5893-8 (eBook)

Center for Strategic & International Studies
1616 Rhode Island Avenue, NW
Washington, DC 20036
202-887-0200 | www.csis.org

Rowman & Littlefield
4501 Forbes Boulevard
Lanham, MD 20706
301-459-3366 | www.rowman.com

Contents

| Acknowledgments

The author wishes to thank Heather Conley, Jeffrey Rathke, Camille Grand, Richard Nephew, François Rivasseau, Nicolas Pillerel, and Caroline Rohloff for their very helpful comments on earlier drafts of this report and CSIS Europe Program's interns Sriram Ramesh and Anna Olevsky for their help in editing it.

This report is made possible by general support to CSIS. No direct sponsorship contributed to its publication.

Executive Summary

- Transatlantic sanctions adopted against Russia, a strategy of hard power coercion short of the use of force, have enabled Europe and the United States, along with their allies like Canada, Japan, and Australia, to build a united response to Russia's strategy of militarized destabilization in Ukraine. This achievement was possible even as the interpretation of the origins of the crisis in Ukraine and conclusions to draw from it differed between the European Union and the United States but even more so among Europeans. For many of them, Europe should neither accept Russia's fait accompli policy in Ukraine nor fully isolate itself from Russia.

- Transatlantic sanctions imposed a real cost on the Russian economy in 2014 and in the first half of 2015. Although this cost is hard to disentangle from the fall in oil prices and the poor management of the Russian economy in recent years, sanctions are believed to have cut Russia's real GDP by more than 1 percent between the summer of 2014 and the summer of 2015, contributing significantly to the recession currently experienced by the Russian economy. Russians acknowledge the impact of sanctions but still support Russia's actions in Ukraine as President Putin's popularity has increased in the past year.

- Even as sanctions cost Russia a lot, they are also impacting European economies significantly. Europe-Russia trade—about €285 billion in 2014 and €326 billion in 2013 in two-way trade—is expected to decline sharply in 2015: a 30 percent decline would be in line with the data available for the first six months of the year. Europe-Russia trade could therefore shrink by about €80 billion in 2015 and cost Europe about €30 billion in lost exports to Russia. Those amounts are significantly higher than what Iran sanctions cost the European economy in the past decade, and markedly greater than the cost to the U.S. economy of Russia sanctions. This could complicate the support for sanctions over time in Europe. U.S. policymakers should acknowledge the price to their European partners; transatlantic solidarity on sanctions would be undermined if Europeans perceived that the United States was outsourcing to its allies the lion's share of the cost of handling the crisis.

- Despite their impact on the Russian economy, transatlantic sanctions have not altered Russia's strategy to use military force to destabilize Ukraine and retain influence over its future. But sanctions have likely pushed Russia toward negotiating the conclusion of the Minsk ceasefire agreements and to a certain extent implementing them. Despite frequent violations, the Minsk II agreement concluded in February 2015 remains the only pathway currently on the table toward a long-term political settlement.

- As demonstrated by the nuclear deal reached by the P5+1 countries with Iran on July 14, 2015, sanctions do not get sanctioned countries to renounce their strategic objectives, but do force them to compromise when used by sanctioning countries as leverage in a negotiation. Sanctions will not solve the crisis in Ukraine by themselves—only if they can be used as leverage by the sanctioning countries, the West, to define with Russia and Ukraine a mutual way forward.

- Although being constrained by Europe's economic interconnection to Russia, transatlantic sanctions can in that context play a role in buying Ukraine time for domestic consolidation and reform and in helping to achieve a compromise as long as they follow realistic objectives and can be sustained over time. To that end, the European Union and the United States must continue to work hand-in-hand and should:

  - Refuse any kinds of sanctions relief as long as a true ceasefire does not hold in Ukraine for several months in a row. Such a ceasefire requires the implementation of all security parameters of the Minsk II agreement and additional monitoring on the ground.

  - Stand ready to respond positively and quickly if Russia's behavior changes in Ukraine enabling a solid ceasefire to be installed, even if the situation falls short of the full implementation of the Minsk II agreement and cannot immediately enable Kiev to restore full control of its border with Russia. However, sanctions relief should remain minimal and reversible as long as Ukraine's full sovereignty over its territory, including direct border control in eastern Ukraine and a negotiated settlement of the situation in Crimea, isn't restored.

  - Prepare to increase pressure against Russia by the beginning of 2016, when the Minsk II agreement is supposed to be fully implemented, if a sustainable ceasefire still isn't in place at the time. Additional smart sanctions—which should focus on constraining Russia's financial room for maneuver rather than further cutting trade between Europe and Russia—could also be required if the security situation significantly deteriorates before that deadline, for instance, if the separatist groups launch a new offensive.

  - Recognize that increased sanctions against Russia would be a tough challenge for Europe, considering the different perspectives and interests they have on the ongoing crisis. At least, Europeans should sustain sanctions over a longer time than initially expected by putting in place creative solidarity mechanisms.

  - Increase support to the Ukrainian government's reform efforts, whose success will be key to convince Europeans that sustaining sanctions is worth it. The role of sanctions will be radically transformed if Ukraine collapses, even becoming possibly pointless.

  - Focus the use of sanctions against Russia on its destabilizing activities in Ukraine. Deterrence, defense, and civilian measures, rather than sanctions, should be the West's priority in ensuring the security of NATO member states. Sanctions are meant to address Russia's behavior in Ukraine, not what Russia has become. Eventually lifting sanctions would not, and will not, mean returning to business as usual.

| Introduction

To many officials in Europe and in the United States, Russia's annexation of Crimea in February 2014 and the subsequent conflict in eastern Ukraine came as a shock. Russia's blatant violation of Ukraine's sovereignty and the foundational principles of post–Cold War peace was a complete blindside. On-the-ground, immediate military opposition to Russian incursions, however, was not a realistic option.

Ukraine is not a NATO ally and assurances such as the 1994 Budapest Memorandum are politically more than legally binding. Although Russia's aggression was politically unacceptable, the transatlantic alliance has no legal obligation to defend Ukraine's sovereignty militarily. And Western leaders quickly discarded the option, considering the underlying risks of a military escalation between the West and Russia. Russia understood this hesitancy well and made sure, through multiple statements by President Putin, to impress upon Western countries how much escalation could cost— even the consideration of having nuclear weapons playing a role in the crisis—if they considered interfering militarily in Ukraine.

With military coercive options constrained, and public condemnations considered inadequate in light of the severity of the situation, hard power economic coercion in the form of sanctions quickly emerged as a realistic response to hold Russia accountable and to deter it from escalating the conflict further. While the first sanctions adopted in the aftermath of the annexation of Crimea in March 2014 focused on individual sanctions, increasing violence in eastern Ukraine and the attack perpetrated on the civilian aircraft MH17 yielded broader sectorial sanctions in the summer of 2014.

Since then, ceasefire agreements were negotiated in Minsk, Belarus, in September 2014 and in February 2015. While the September 2014 Minsk I ceasefire quickly collapsed due to renewed hostilities last winter, the February 2015 Minsk II ceasefire, brokered by France and Germany, managed to temporarily reduce the violence. However, since the implementation of Minsk II, the Organization for Security and Cooperation in Europe (OSCE), which is in charge of monitoring the ceasefire, has reported daily violations.

After almost a year of significant economic sanctions, the situation in eastern Ukraine is far from stable, balancing precariously between the possibility of new full-scale hostilities and the prospect of a long-term frozen conflict—sustained by Russia through its support to separatists and rebels groups. Lately, an additional ceasefire declared on September 1 seems to be holding better but it remains fragile.

Despite the significant cost of the sectorial sanctions for the European economy, the European Union agreed to renew the most significant sanctions against Russia, originally due to expire at the end of July 2015, for a full semester, until January 2016. The Europeans' ability to sustain, or even intensify, sanctions against Russia, if the situation on the ground warrants it, will be a challenge. Many experts and officials, including the EU High Representative Federica Mogherini, have publicly challenged the notion that sanctions can realistically help secure a long-term diplomatic settlement in Ukraine, and suggest that lessons drawn from the use of economic coercion against Iran are irrelevant when dealing with Russia.

Because of its weaker economic relationship with Russia, it should be less politically challenging for the United States to maintain its sanctions against Russia over the long term. This, however, raises a serious coordination issue within a transatlantic alliance that has managed for now to remain broadly united on how to deal with the situation in Ukraine and more broadly with Russia itself, in particular in the NATO context.

At this critical juncture, this report provides a comprehensive assessment of the impact of sanctions against Russia since their adoption and progressive reinforcement in 2014. It also makes policy recommendations as to what Europeans and Americans should do next, depending on several scenarios.

The report begins by explaining how sanctions contributed to strengthening unity within the transatlantic community, analyzes the economic impact sanctions have had on the Russian and European economies, and examines the impact sanctions have played on Russia's behavior.

Based on this assessment, the report concludes that sanctions can be useful in facilitating the establishment of a long-term diplomatic settlement in Ukraine, so long as Western countries are prepared to sustain them in the long run and use them with flexibility, including by contemplating early but minimal sanctions relief in case the ceasefire should hold more durably in eastern Ukraine (with a "snap-back" provision against backsliding).

The report also recommends, if sanctions needed to be increased, that they target Russia's financial sector instead of further cutting Western trade with Russia. These sanctions would hurt Russia more, considering its potential constraints in accessing foreign exchange reserves, while being more appealing to Europe, thereby limiting the possible dissatisfaction with sanctions and making them more sustainable. In doing so, the United States and the European Union would still need to tread carefully so that risks associated with Russia's financial destabilization could be contained.

Finally, the report advocates for now focusing the use of sanctions against Russia on Russia's destabilizing behavior in Ukraine, although sanctions could provide Europeans and Americans another option to deal with hybrid threats posed to European security by Russia's new assertiveness.

1 | Achievements of Transatlantic Sanctions against Russia over Past Year

Sanctions' Strengthening of Transatlantic Unity around Hard Power Economic Coercion in Absence of Credible Military Options

Resorting to sanctions against Russia reflected, first and foremost, the need and desire to build internal unity both within the European Union and between the European Union and the United States to reject Russia's initiatives in Ukraine. Policymakers, in Europe and in the United States, quickly identified sanctions as the optimal tool to respond to Russia's violations of Ukraine's sovereignty and retain flexibility for adapting to a volatile situation.

As explained on March 17, 2014, by a senior official from the U.S. administration in a background briefing, "President Obama has been very clear since the Russian intervention in Crimea that we, together with our European allies, would be imposing costs on Russia for its violation of Ukraine's sovereignty and territorial integrity even as we have made clear our openness to a diplomatic pathway to de-escalation."[1]

Sanctions were considered a common denominator around which to rally among the hard power coercive options available in defining the West's reaction. There was indeed no political will to consider military options to oppose Russia's involvement in Ukraine. This reflected the fact that both Europe and the United States, contrary to Russia, did not see their strategic interests to be so threatened in Ukraine to justify resorting to the use of force. Early in the crisis, President Barack Obama was clear that a military option in Ukraine[2] could not be contemplated, a stance wholeheartedly agreed to by his European counterparts.

It made sense that both NATO and EU member states would not defend militarily a country with which they were not bound by defense guarantees, or even security assurances. For instance, U.S. and UK obligations under the 1994 Budapest Memorandum did not go as far as to foresee a military involvement in case of a threat

---

[1] The White House, "Background Briefing by Senior Administration Officials on Ukraine," March 17, 2014, https://www.whitehouse.gov/the-press-office/2014/03/17/background-briefing-senior-administration-officials-ukraine.

[2] See multiple interviews President Obama gave early in 2014, such as the interview with Mark Mullen from NBC San Diego affiliate in which the president argued, "We are not going to be getting into a military excursion in Ukraine.... I think even the Ukrainians would acknowledge that for us to engage Russia militarily would not be appropriate, and wouldn't be good for Ukraine either."

against Ukraine's security, simply that they would "seek immediate United Nations Security Council (UNSC) action to provide assistance to Ukraine."[3]

Many experts pointed out that discarding a military option from the outset may have weakened the West's position by signaling to Moscow that Russia would retain its position of escalation dominance. It is very unlikely that European public opinions, or the American public opinion for that matter, would have supported a military confrontation against Russia for the sake of Crimea, nor even for Ukraine.

But for sure, all military options do not necessarily equate to a military confrontation with Russia. The debate about whether the United States, in coordination with its European allies, should deliver more military assistance, especially nonlethal and lethal weaponry, has been ongoing almost since the beginning of the crisis.[4] The Obama administration has made its skepticism clear about the limited added value it saw in such deliveries, against the views of many in the U.S. security establishment but in line with those of most of its European allies.[5]

Whether the West relying more than it did on limited military options could have prevented the crisis to escalate in 2014 after the annexation of Crimea is an open question. Whether promoting limited military options would achieve that same goal today is another. Ultimately, the answer to this question depends on what one sees as being Ukraine's strategic interests. Ukraine needs to reform and consolidate. So while military assistance may be useful to reinforce Ukraine's ability to defend itself in the future, it will be counterproductive if it is used today to entertain a war in eastern Ukraine that Moscow will not allow Kiev to win militarily anyway.

In the absence of a significant military component to the West's reaction, sanctions managed to reconcile contradictory objectives among Europeans. Eastern European allies like Poland and the Baltic States and member states, such as the United Kingdom or Sweden, along with Washington and Ottawa, quickly attempted to push their partners to isolate Russia from the European Union through strong sanctions. Central and Southern European member states such as Hungary, Slovakia, and Greece showed skepticism about adopting sanctions but did not block them. In the middle, Germany, France, and other key players such as the Netherlands acknowledged the justification of targeted economic sanctions but promoted a response that would retain open communication channels and economic relations in order not to fully isolate Europe from its most significant and powerful eastern neighbor.

In spite of these different approaches, consensus was built around the creation of a limited but still significant sanctions regime to respond to Russia's transgressions. All

---

[3] Memorandum on Security Assurances in Connection with Ukraine's accession to the Treaty on the Non-Proliferation of Nuclear Weapons, December 5, 1994.

[4] See, for instance, Ivo Daalder et al., "Preserving Ukraine's Independence, Resisting Russian Aggression: What the United States and NATO Must Do," Atlantic Council, February 2015, http://www.thechicagocouncil.org/sites/default/files/UkraineReport_February2015_FINAL.pdf.

[5] Nancy A. Youssef and Noah Shachtman, "Pentagon: Team Obama Is Too Timid on Russia," *Daily Beast*, August 6, 2015, http://www.thedailybeast.com/articles/2015/08/06/pentagon-team-obama-is-too-timid-on-putin.html.

transatlantic partners rejected Russia's fait accompli policy in Ukraine, and looked to deter further initiatives in the same vein. They also reassured Eastern European allies about the strength of solidarity within the European Union. To be sure, sanctions checked many boxes.

Sanctions' Significant Economic Cost to Russia's Economy and Collateral Damage to Europe's Economies

Contrary to the vision sometimes entertained,[6] the sanctions adopted in 2014 have not been designed to isolate Russia from the West in the same way that sanctions isolated Iran, North Korea, or Cuba. This has been a misconception, considering the higher degree of integration of the Russian economy into global markets and even more importantly, the stronger economic relations between Europe and Russia.[7] Likewise, the decision made by G7 countries to exclude Russia from the G8 was a symbolic, political sanction, not a recognition that the international community could really afford to deal with world affairs and international crises in Iran, Syria, or anywhere Russia has obvious national interests involved, without taking Russia's positions into consideration.

Disagreements over Russia's support to the Bashar Assad regime in the civil war in Syria preceded sanctions and have continued after their imposition, even more so now that Russia's military presence in Syria seems to be on the rise. Moscow maintained a constructive participation in the P5+1 nuclear negotiation with Iran even after sanctions had been imposed. Cooperation, competition, or confrontation on international crises beyond Ukraine will remain dictated by Western and Russian interests, rather than by the fate of Ukraine-related sanctions. Likewise, the fate of Ukraine-related sanctions should only be determined by facts on the ground in Ukraine, not by the West's interest to cooperate with Russia on other crises, for instance in Syria.

Rather than isolating Russia, sanctions were designed to achieve a targeted economic impact on the Russian economy that would not destabilize the entire international financial system, but would still provide an incentive for Moscow to negotiate a settlement to the crisis in Ukraine. As underlined by then-U.S. undersecretary of the treasury for terrorism and financial intelligence, David Cohen, the Russia sanctions program required an "innovative approach"[8] and the United States and Europe had to

---

[6] See, for instance, Suzanne Nossel, "It's Time to Kill the Feel-Good Myth of Sanctions," *Foreign Policy*, June 9, 2015, http://foreignpolicy.com/2015/06/09/its-time-to-kill-the-feel-good-myth-of-sanctions-russia-iran/.

[7] According to European Commission figures publicly made available by the Directorate General for Trade, Iran represented about 1 percent of the EU external trade in 2004, before the first European sanctions were implemented. Russia, in the meantime, accounted for 7 percent of the EU global exports and 12 percent of its global imports in 2013.

[8] U.S. Department of Treasury, "Remarks of Under Secretary for Terrorism and Financial Intelligence David Cohen at The Practicing Law Institute's 'Coping with U.S. Export Controls and Sanctions' Seminar, 'The Evolution of U.S. Financial Power,'" November 12, 2014, http://www.treasury.gov/press-center/press-releases/Pages/jl9716.aspx.

find "a way to increase the pressure sufficiently to affect Moscow's calculations while minimizing the risk to global financial markets, global energy supplies, and overall economic activity in the United States and Europe." The result has been the creation of targeted, or "surgical," sanctions against Russia, measures that would not "push Russia onto its knees," in the words of French President Hollande.[9] The idea of creating sectorial sanctions—that is, measures imposed on specific companies because of their activities in particular areas of the economy—derived from that logic. This innovation was not entirely new, as its use had already been contemplated against Iran, but eventually not implemented in that context.

A significant impact on the Russian economy, even if Russians continue to support President Putin's policy in Ukraine.

Sanctions impacted an economy structurally in bad shape, as its main macroeconomic indicators showed even before the sanctions were imposed.[10] The European Commission estimated in an October 2014 study[11] that the sanctions would cut Russian GDP growth by 0.6 point in 2014 and 1.1 point in 2015. The International Monetary Fund (IMF) recently brought credibility to these figures, evaluating that "model-based estimates suggest that sanctions and counter-sanctions could initially reduce Russia's real GDP by 1 to 1-1/2 percent."[12] Prior to sanctions, Russia's GDP had increased by a small 1.6 percent in 2013, a level much below comparable emerging economies like India or China.

The World Bank expected Russia's real GDP to grow slightly, by 0.6 percent in 2014, but would suffer a contraction of 3.8 percent in 2015 and 0.3 percent in 2016. More recent estimates by the World Bank, based on a more optimistic average oil price in 2015 and 2016, projects a smaller-than-expected recession of 2.7 percent of real GDP in 2015, but a growth of 0.7 percent in 2016 and 2.5 percent in 2017.[13] A comparison of the European Commission, IMF, and World Bank estimates shows that sanctions are significantly contributing to the Russian economic recession in 2015. Without sanctions, Russia's real GDP would contract by only 1.6 percent.[14]

Russia's most significant Achilles' heel was the risk of a liquidity crisis, and this is exactly what sanctions cleverly targeted: financial sectorial sanctions affected non-state companies' debt and companies, which in turn put pressure on the government

---

[9] Interview with the French radio France Inter, January 5, 2015.

[10] For a comprehensive and updated description of the state of Russia's economy in 2015, see World Bank, "Russia Economic Report 33: The Dawn of an Economic Era," April 2015, http://www.worldbank.org/en/news/press-release/2015/04/01/russia-economic-report-33. This report includes a section on the impact of sanctions on the Russian economy.

[11] This study has not been publicly released but was circulated to member states at that time.

[12] International Monetary Fund, "Russian Federation: 2015 Article IV Consultation," Country Report No. 15/211, August 2015, http://www.imf.org/external/pubs/ft/scr/2015/cr15211.pdf.

[13] World Bank latest estimates released on June 1, 2015, http://www.worldbank.org/en/news/press-release/2015/06/01/world-bank-revises-its-growth-projections-for-russia-for-2015-and-2016. For the earlier growth estimates, see World Bank, "Russia Economic Report 33: The Dawn of an Economic Era."

[14] This estimation calculated by the author is only indicative, as informal figures from the European Commission cannot be exactly compared with other figures provided by the World Bank, both institutions being unlikely to base their estimations on the exact same parameters.

for access to the state's foreign exchange reserves (as the energy company Rosneft has tried to do in recent months, for instance). According to the World Bank, sanctions have indeed had the greatest impact on destabilizing the Russian foreign exchange market and the falling ruble, due to restrictions on Russia's access to international financial markets, as well as the degradation of consumer and investor confidence.

Such a mechanism, along with low oil prices and reduced access to international capital markets, caused a significant devaluation of the ruble at the end of 2014. Although it has stabilized since then, the ruble lost 45 percent of its value against the dollar in 2014. Monetary interventions to support the ruble have reduced Russia's international reserves, decreasing from upwards of $475 billion in June 2014 to nearly $360 billion in March 2015. According to President Putin, they have since stabilized at around $360 billion, largely due to more favorable oil prices,[15] but the situation could be made difficult again in the near future by the recent drop in the ruble or by a further decline of oil prices. In all logic, the upcoming reintroduction in 2016 of greater volumes of Iranian crude oil in international markets, due to the lifting of sanctions against Iran deriving from the July 14 nuclear deal, should contribute to maintaining low oil prices.

Sectorial financial sanctions that limit Russia's access to international capital markets are likely to have long-term effects, as the lack of capital will weaken Russia's long-term growth potential. Sanctions targeting European exports to Russia, in either the energy technologies, the dual-use technologies, or the defense sectors, may not be so quickly effective against Russia, while imposing a more immediate cost on European exporters (in August 2014, for instance, the export of sensitive technologies for frontier oil projects declined 64 percent compared to August 2013 and 71 percent compared to July 2014). They will, however, have a longer-term impact, as the lack of Western technologies (which will not be easily substituted) will cripple these sectors' ability to maintain their production capacities.

In addition to purely economic consequences, sanctions also impacted Russia's ambitious plans for the modernization of its military. Things could possibly get worse in the years ahead. This impact has so far been twofold. On one hand, Russia's declining public budget has imposed measures to delay investments in modernization projects.[16] More importantly, on the other hand, sectorial European sanctions against the Russian military industry and Ukraine's own decision to ban military exports to Russia are causing delays in the Russian navy's shipbuilding plan *inter alia*.[17] Russia's ability to find substitutes to replace Ukrainian-made gas turbine engines may be

---

[15] Figures provided by Bloomberg Business available at http://www.bloomberg.com/quote/RUREFEG:IND and confirmed by President Putin during a speech made at the 19th St Petersburg International Economic Forum: "According to my information, our reserves came to $361.6 billion as of June 5. They are very slightly lower now, because some money has been used."

[16] Matthew Bodner and Anna Dolgov, "Putin Warns Russian Defense Industry Not to Fall Behind," *The Moscow Times*, July 19, 2015; and Alex Lockie, "Russia's huge military upgrade hit another snag—and Putin is not happy," *Business Insider*, July 17, 2015, http://www.businessinsider.com/russias-huge-military-upgrade-hit-another-snag-and-putin-is-not-happy-2015-7.

[17] Franz-Stefan Gady, "How the Ukraine Crisis Interrupts Putin's Naval Dreams," *The Diplomat*, June 12, 2015.

questionable in the short term. Such disruptions to the military industry supply chains may be overcome but represent today an obstacle to Russia's modernization plans, which have rarely been fully implemented in the recent past.

The Russian public recognizes the economic impact sanctions are having in Russia. Recent data released by the Pew Research Center,[18] built on a survey conducted in Russia in early 2015, suggests that 45 percent of those polled believe sanctions to have a major effect on the Russian economy, and 33 percent blame Western sanctions for Russia's economic struggles (33 percent blame falling oil prices, while only 25 percent believe current government policies to be responsible for the current economic situation). In addition, 73 percent acknowledge that Russia's economic situation is worsening, up from 44 percent who held that view a year ago.

But instead of turning Russians against their government's policy in Ukraine, sanctions have not prevented them from supporting President Putin even more. The 2015 Pew Research Center data indicates that 88 percent in Russia have confidence in President Putin "to do the right thing regarding world affairs," while only 37 percent acknowledge that his handling of the Ukraine crisis "had led to worsening international opinion of Russia." Even more strikingly, 50 percent believe that Western countries are "most to blame for the violence in eastern Ukraine," while a mere 4 percent blame pro-Russian separatists in Ukraine, and only 2 percent blame Russia itself for the crisis. Altogether, these polls indicate that most Russians do not hold their government responsible for the crisis unfolding in Ukraine, instead blaming the West. Moreover, the Russian government uses sanctions as a scapegoat for Russia's current economic struggles, including those that derive from its poor management.

A real impact on European economies, while the cost of Russia's countermeasures has been manageable.

Assessing the role of sanctions in addressing the Ukrainian crisis must include a cost-benefit analysis of the costs borne by the imposing countries, in relation to the security benefits gained. According to estimates made by the European Commission in October 2014, Russia sanctions made EU real GDP to be lower in 2014 and 2015, by 0.3 percentage points, than it otherwise would have been without sanctions.[19] This impact is not marginal for the European economy, which was supposed to grow by only 1.3 percent in 2014 while the eurozone GDP is expected to grow by 1.5 percent in 2015. These macroeconomic figures may underestimate more severe effects in specific sectors impacted by the sanctions, such as dual-use goods and technologies, the defense sector, or energy-related technologies.

---

[18] See Katie Simmons, Bruce Stokes, and Jacob Poushter, "NATO Publics Blame Russia for Ukrainian Crisis, But Reluctant to Provide Military Aid: In Russia, Anti-Western Views and Support for Putin Surge," Pew Research Center, June 2015, http://www.pewglobal.org/files/2015/06/Pew-Research-Center-Russia-Ukraine-Report-FINAL-June-10-2015.pdf.

[19] Laurence Norman, "EU Projects Impact of Sanctions on Russian Economy," *Wall Street Journal*, October 29, 2014, http://www.wsj.com/articles/eu-projects-impact-of-sanctions-on-russian-economy-1414583901. These figures were confirmed to the author by various sources close to the European Commission.

taken in the framework of the Trilateral Contact Group,[26] although its full implementation remains a challenge still under discussion. The situation is somehow calmer since the entry into force on September 1 of an informal ceasefire. Between September 1 and September 10, the OSCE reported "only" 11 violations a day, on average. The situation remains unstable and quite volatile on the ground, although fears of another Russia-supported large-scale rebel offensive did not materialize during the summer.

Generally speaking, the work of the Trilateral Contact Group remains hampered by the Russian temptation and tactic to make of the whole situation a purely internal Ukrainian issue, making of the separatists Kiev's only interlocutor and making sure Russia doesn't appear to be a direct part in the conflict, but rather a mediator in the conflict's resolution like France and Germany. Meanwhile, the implementation of the "political" side of the Minsk II agreement remains as fragile as the security situation on the ground. Ukraine's Parliament voted on August 31 on potential amendments to the Constitution, granting more power to the country's rebel-held regions. But this reform lacks support in Kiev because it may grant too much power to the eastern provinces, and lacks support in Moscow for the opposite reason that such powers don't give rebels—and Russia—sufficient clout over Kiev's politics.

This reality reflects a simple fact: Russia's authorities, and President Putin in particular, consider that the political value created for them by the continuation of Russia's strategy in Ukraine has so far offset the economic and political costs imposed by sanctions. Sanctions have not deterred Russia's military involvement in Ukraine, as recently illustrated in a report released by the Atlantic Council, based on open-source information that presented a comprehensive picture of Russia's supply of troops and weapons in Ukraine.[27] Likewise, U.S. Army Europe commander, Ben Hodges, asserted the active presence of 12,000 Russian soldiers in eastern Ukraine,[28] although U.S. officials have subsequently avoided citing such specific figure.

U.S. defense secretary Ashton Carter had it exactly right when he said, on his way back from a recent trip in Europe, that "what's clear is that sanctions are working on the Russian economy. . . What's not apparent is that that effect on his economy is deterring Putin from following the course that was evidenced last year in Crimea."[29] The overall state of both the Ukraine crisis and the diplomatic process aimed at handling it remain nothing but fragile.

---

[26] The Trilateral Contact Group is composed of Russian, Ukrainian, and OSCE officials and intends, through working groups, to make progress on the implementation of several aspects of the Minsk agreements.

[27] Maksymilian Czuperski et al., "Hiding in Plain Sight, Putin's War in Ukraine," Atlantic Council, Washington, DC, May 2015.

[28] Sabine Siebold and Caroline Copley, "Some 12,000 Russian soldiers in Ukraine supporting rebels: U.S. commander," Reuters, March 3, 2015, http://www.reuters.com/article/2015/03/03/us-ukraine-russia-soldiers-idUSKBN0LZ2FV20150303.

[29] David J. Lynch, "Carter Says Sanctions Alone Aren't Deterring Russia in Ukraine," *Bloomberg Business*, June 5, 2015, http://www.bloomberg.com/news/articles/2015-06-05/carter-says-sanctions-alone-aren-t-deterring-russia-in-ukraine.

2 | Future of Sanctions against Russia

Case for Sustaining Sanctions against Russia, Despite Their Costs and Limitations

Sanctions skeptics are keen to underline the significant limits of sanctions imposed on Russia. Indeed, Russia sanctions have intrinsic limitations that reduce the efficiency of their use and their ability to alter Russia's course of action in Ukraine. They should not be overstated, though.

Europe and Russia are reciprocally too vulnerable.

As European trade with Russia was already significantly reduced in 2014 and is expected to be even more so in 2015, there will be a political limit to the economic cost European countries can accept. This limit is not predetermined and will also depend on the evolution of the situation on the ground. A greater cost will be more difficult to bear if the situation appears to remain "under control" in eastern Ukraine, that is, in the kind of low-intensity conflictive reported since the conclusion of the Minsk II agreement in February 2015.

Likewise, even if the facts on the ground require tougher measures and EU and U.S. leaders can find a consensus, Europeans may be self-deterred to tighten sanctions due to the consequences a liquidity crisis in Russia would likely have on global financial markets, and in turn on them. Europeans could also be afraid of new Russian countermeasures, but Russia's room for maneuver should not be overestimated. Russia has and will continue to have significant constraints in the countermeasures it can impose on Europe. Cutting Russian hydrocarbons exports to Europe would likely hurt Russia more than Europe itself, considering Moscow's dependency to European payments for Russian gas and oil. At the end of the day, Europe may be less vulnerable to further cuts in its economic relations with Russia than the opposite.

Long-term sustainability of sanctions in Europe is challenging.

If sanctions contributed to building unity around a collective answer to Russia, they also created frustrations within the European Union about the cost they represented for the European economy. As described earlier, three groups of EU member states formed themselves around the issue, one of them being openly hostile to the sanctions. Greece's prime minister declared in Moscow on April 8, 2015, "we openly disapproved of the sanctions. It is not an efficient solution. We think it could bring about a new cold war between Russia and the west."[30] On June 2, 2015, Slovakia's

---

[30] Shaun Walker, "Alexis Tsipras in Moscow asks Europe to end sanctions against Russia," *The Guardian*, April 8, 2015, http://www.theguardian.com/world/2015/apr/08/alexis-tsipras-in-moscow-asks-europe-to-end-sanctions-against-russia.

prime minister, Robert Fico, also stated in Moscow that "sanctions do not have the expected effect. They harm both Europe and Russia."[31] Although such frustrations led to bitter public statements, they rarely resulted in formal positions opposing sanctions in Brussels when the issue came to the EU agenda. Therefore, they could be read as attempts to sit on the fence, sending friendly messages to Russia, with which serious economic interests and ties must be protected, without jeopardizing European unity at the end of the day.

It should therefore not come as a surprise that the decision taken in June 2015 to extend European sanctions until January 2016 did not even require a debate among EU foreign affairs ministers. European Union decisionmaking involves legal rules of voting on the one hand[32] and politics on the other. Sanctions usually require unanimous votes by all member states, thereby legally granting a single member state the ability to oppose their adoption (or renewal in this instance). Politically, though, it is unrealistic to expect small member states to be able to block consensus without the support of a coalition involving at least one of the bigger member states. Russia could certainly be willing to exploit a few member states' interests in Russia to push them to oppose the renewal of sanctions in Brussels. But this tactic has so far proved inefficient. Europeans, on the contrary, have proved up to the challenge by maintaining unity.

Russia is going to adapt to sanctions and may partially overcome their effects through commercial and financial diversification.

By pointing to the use of the Eurasian Economic Union and more intensive cooperation with China, sanctions skeptics rightly underline Russian efforts to better protect itself against external economic pressure from the West by diversifying partnerships. A good example of this strategy was the October 2014 signing of 38 agreements between Russia and China in different areas of cooperation. One of these agreements was made between both countries' central banks to create a three-year yuan-ruble swap mechanism that could give Russia more flexibility to access international financing and escape liquidity shortage.[33] Similar efforts may be undergoing to reduce Russia's vulnerabilities to Western institutions and generally speaking to Western economic warfare, such as the creation by the BRICS (Brazil,

---

[31] "Fico critical of Russia sanctions in Moscow," *The Slovak Spectator*, June 3, 2015, http://spectator.sme.sk/c/20057742/fico-talked-relations-with-ukraine-from-moscow.html.

[32] Articles 28 of the Treaty on European Union establishes that "Where the international situation requires operational action by the Union, the Council shall adopt the necessary decisions. They shall lay down their objectives, scope, the means to be made available to the Union, if necessary their duration, and the conditions for their implementation." Article 31 adds: "Decisions under this Chapter shall be taken by the European Council and the Council acting unanimously, except where this Chapter provides otherwise." Unanimity isn't a golden rule; for instance, the Council could act by qualified majority "when adopting a decision defining a Union action or position, on a proposal which the High Representative . . . has presented following a specific request from the European Council, made on its own initiative or that of the High Representative." The usual practice remains in any cases to adopt sanctions decisions following the rule of unanimity.

[33] Vladimir Kutzenov and Olga Tanas, "Russia, China Sign Currency Swap Agreement to Double $100b Trade," *Bloomberg Business*, October 13, 2014, http://www.bloomberg.com/news/articles/2014-10-13/russia-china-sign-currency-swap-agreement-to-double-100b-trade.

Russia, India, China and South Africa) group of a New Development Bank (NDB),[34] with capital of $100 billion, aimed at financing investments. Russian companies could benefit from loans made by the NDB, although no formal projects have been announced for now. Likewise, the Chinese ability to provide Russia with sufficiently advanced technology and equipment in the energy sector remains an open question, as China hasn't been able yet to do so for Iran, despite Iranian urgent needs in modernizing oil production technologies.

Role of Sanctions in Resolving Crisis in Ukraine If Related to Realistic Objectives and Sustainability

While Russia sanctions have limitations, there are still reasons to believe that sanctions can be an important asset to help resolve the crisis in Ukraine, as long as they are set with realistic objectives and used strategically in line with the evolution of the situation on the ground.

Set sanctions with realistic objectives and principles.

As the Iran case has recently shown, sanctions only alter marginally fundamental choices made by sovereign states about their security—although requiring a country that faces the world's most unstable region to renounce nuclear weapons it doesn't yet have is far more demanding than asking a nuclear weapon state to stop invading one of its weak neighbors who chose 20 years ago to get rid of its nuclear weapons. Despite all the sanctions imposed against Iran over the years, the Iranian regime has not renounced the technical infrastructure and capability to enrich uranium, a prerequisite to acquire a nuclear weapon if it needs to one day. However, over the years, sanctions did force Iran to better take into account Western interests and concerns. Eventually, sanctions led Iran to compromise through the Comprehensive Joint Plan of Action agreed with the P5+1 group in Vienna on July 14, 2015. Sanctions forced a compromise, not a capitulation. Stronger sanctions against Iran may have led to an even more favorable agreement for the West, but not likely to Iran's acceptance of a full dismantlement of its uranium enrichment capacities.

Eventually, the same question will need to be posed in the Russia context. In March 2015, EU heads of state made the decision to link the lifting of EU sanctions with the full implementation of the Minsk II agreement.[35] Establishing this link was useful as it set, for the first time since the beginning of the crisis in early 2014, a concrete objective to sanctions. But this also has limits, as a full implementation of the Minsk agreements remains unlikely in the near future, which could in turn impose the continuation of sanctions over a long period of time.

---

[34] Kathrin Hille, "Sanctions-scarred Russian groups eye Bric finance options," *Financial Times*, July 7, 2015, http://www.ft.com/intl/cms/s/0/20275444-24ec-11e5-9c4e-a775d2b173ca.html#axzz3hsKBvbzq.
[35] As stated by Donald Tusk, the European Council president, on March 19, 2015, EU heads of state agreed to "align our sanctions regime to the implementation of the Minsk agreements" and "that the duration of economic sanctions will be clearly linked to the complete implementation of the Minsk agreements, bearing in mind that this is only foreseen by the end of 2015." Remarks by President Donald Tusk after the first session of the European Council meeting, Brussels, March 19, 2015.

Although many Western leaders rightly rejected the idea of Russian spheres of influence as an anachronistic way to restrict Ukraine's strategic choices, influence in itself over partners, allies, and adversaries remains a basic principle of statecraft in today's international relations. Considering history and geography, it is inevitable that Russia will continue to have some influence over Ukraine as a major player in the neighborhood, but the modalities of this relationship will need to be rethought in light of Russian behavior in recent years. Ideally, Russia would need to be brought back into a path where it sees peaceful influence as a realistic way to protect its interests in Ukraine, even if Russia shows little inclination to follow such a path for now, and Russia's military intervention in Ukraine has by now weakened Ukraine's tolerance for any kind of Russian influence.

An eventual pragmatic solution can only be built around a real ceasefire giving Ukraine time and political space to grow stronger. Here are a few principles around which a more realistic and flexible approach could be built:

- *There shall be no sanctions relief as long as a true ceasefire does not hold in Ukraine.* The Minsk II agreement combined security/military-centered measures and more political considerations.[36] The security/military parameters of this agreement[37] are the most relevant parameters to the use of sanctions because 1) sanctions are first and foremost a tool for security and 2) it is on the security situation that Russia has direct leverage (while trying in the meantime to gain more on the political one). It should be clear that no sanctions will be suspended or lifted as long as a ceasefire based on the security parameters outlined in the Minsk II agreement does not hold for several months in a row and cannot be confirmed on the ground by the OSCE Monitoring Mission.

  Having said that, the prospect of suspending a minimal part of the sanctions in place should be contemplated if the implementation of the security/military parameters of the Minsk agreement could be satisfactorily achieved. For instance, a limited number of entities designated under the sectorial lists could be delisted after the OSCE had confirmed the absence of ceasefire violations for several months in a row. While these designations would need to be put back in place, or snapped-back, if the ceasefire broke, most of the existing sanctions would remain in force as long as the political parameters of the Minsk II agreement[38] cannot be fully implemented and Ukraine's sovereignty over its full territory be restored. Those requirements would obviously require the

---

[36] Package of Measures for the Implementation of the Minsk Agreements, Minsk, Belarus, February 12, 2015.

[37] Namely: "Immediate and comprehensive ceasefire"; "Withdrawal of all heavy weapons by both sides by equal distances"; "Ensure effective monitoring and verification of the ceasefire"; "Ensure release and exchange of all hostages and unlawfully detained persons"; "Ensure safe access, delivery, storage, and distribution of humanitarian assistance"; "Withdrawal of all foreign armed formations, military equipment, as well as mercenaries."

[38] Namely: Provision related to the organization of "local elections"; "Ensure pardon and amnesty by enacting the law prohibiting prosecution and punishment of persons in connection with the events"; "Definition of modalities of full resumption of socio-economic ties"; "Carrying out constitutional reform in Ukraine."

"reinstatement of full control of the state border by the Government of Ukraine throughout the conflict area." There is no visible path toward returning Crimea to Ukraine's internationally recognized sovereignty, so suspension of Crimea-related sanctions would not be on the table.

Suspending a minimal part of the sanctions in exchange for a more solid and respected ceasefire will be a difficult decision to agree on between Europeans and Americans. Critics will argue that this would institutionalize a frozen conflict in eastern Ukraine and reward a Russian abstention rather than a real change in Russia's policy in Ukraine. Critics will also say that sanctions relief, even minimal, will weaken support for sanctions in both governments and in the private sector by creating expectations for a complete lifting of sanctions. While these arguments are not false, it would still be very difficult politically to justify not changing anything to the sanctions when the situation on the ground would have improved significantly. Plus, the integrity of the sanctions architecture could be maintained until Ukraine regains full control of its border with Russia.

- *Sanctions could increase so long as such true ceasefire does not hold in Ukraine or if the situation further deteriorates.* As Europe and the United States should stand ready to reward good behavior without renouncing principles, they should also draw conclusions from a status quo that would continue to involve daily violations of the ceasefire. As explained at the G7 meeting in Germany in June 2015 by European Council President Donald Tusk, a tough voice on Ukraine within the European Union: "given the current situation, if anyone wants to start a debate about changing the sanctions regime, the discussion could only be about strengthening it."[39] In addition, Europeans and Americans should be prepared to face a significant deterioration resulting in further territorial gains by separatists backed by Russian forces, or even a new "black swan," comparable to the downing of the civilian flight MH17. Deterioration could take place either in eastern Ukraine or elsewhere, for instance at the border between Ukraine and the autonomous region of Transnistria.

Without such obvious deterioration, Europe and the United States should still be ready to increase sanctions against Russia in the absence of a true ceasefire at the deadline foreseen by the Minsk II agreement. The West will need to counter a possible Russian strategy that would consist either on simply playing for time, or more perversely in avoiding significant territorial gains in Ukraine while slowly trying to whittle away small parts of Ukraine's territory. Keeping in mind the political and economic constraints related to the adoption of further sanctions, options to reinforce sanctions could include the following items:

---

[39] Council of the European Union, "Press statement by President Donald Tusk at the press conference before the G7 summit, Schloss Elmau, Germany," June 7, 2015, http://www.consilium.europa.eu/en/press/press-releases/2015/06/7-tusk-statement-g7-press-conference/.

o   A more restrictive implementation of the existing sanctions,[40] coupled with their necessary adaptation to circumvention tactics or to legal challenges.[41] For instance, the United States and the European Union could require Western financial institutions to wait for a minimal amount of time before granting consecutive loans to Russian entities designated under the sectorial lists, thereby preventing continued credit to entities that should only be allowed to benefit from less than 30-day maturity loans.

o   Reinforcing the financial sanctions already in place to increase Russia's difficulties to access financing abroad; the number of Russian entities targeted by existing sanctions against the financing of debts or equities could be extended, while the nature of those sanctions could be slightly worsened: the maturity of debts and equities that Western financial institutions are allowed to finance could be reduced or the scope of the definition of what constitutes a debt or an equity extended, for instance.

o   Further financial measures under the form of blocking sanctions against specific Russian banks could be used but would likely be more difficult for the European Union to accept as they would restrain financial channels used to finance legal trade with Russia.

o   Likewise, aggravating the trade measures in the energy equipment or dual-use domains would likely prove controversial in Europe, as would additional sectorial sanctions against sectors targeted by U.S. Executive Order 13662 (metals, mining, and engineering) but not yet sanctioned.

Other scenarios (signification degradation, "black swan") would likely involve strengthening sanctions even before the December 2015-January 2016 deadline or even stronger sanctions afterwards. Renewed discussion in that case would likely involve, beyond the items presented above, the idea to cut Russia from the Society for Worldwide Interbank Financial Telecommunication (SWIFT) network, the global system for banking orders transmission, and a measure inspired by the Iranian precedent. While Iran was never globally excluded from the network—only Iranian designated financial institutions were formally excluded—the idea to use this instrument against Russia would carry many risks, including a de-legitimization of the company's neutrality as a global provider for financial transactions.

---

[40] Several press articles have underlined the choice made by regulators and operators on both sides of the Atlantic to not implement the strictest sanctions. See, for instance, Kathrin Hille, Jack Farchy, and Courtney Weaver, "Sanctions new normal proves workable for business in Russia," *Financial Times*, June 14, 2015, http://www.ft.com/cms/s/0/98cc653a-110d-11e5-8413-00144feabdc0.html#axzz3kvZ57J2e.
[41] All EU individual sanctions can be challenged before the Court of Justice of the European Union. Accordingly, the Court of Justice is currently reviewing some of the designations pronounced by the European Union against Russian or Ukrainian entities and individuals. In addition to these cases, the "sectorial" designations imposed in the framework of the EU measures against Russia's financial, energy, and defense sectors have also been challenged and should be ruled upon in the coming year.

While Russia and China have already been taking steps toward establishing an independent and less-vulnerable electronic payments network outside of SWIFT, leveraging the company once more against Russia would definitely convince Moscow to set up its own system. What's more, such measures would also run the risk of impacting a large amount of unsanctioned trade, in particular between Europe and Russia, while putting Russia's financial stability in danger, with all global associated risks. Altogether, the costs to cut Russian designated banks from SWIFT could likely outweigh any possible benefits and this measure should therefore be avoided.

Instead, the European Union and the United States could contemplate the following steps:

- As recently suggested by a comprehensive report on the imposition of oil sanctions against Russia,[42] the European Union could reduce its imports of Russian oil, although such a move could expose Europe to additional Russian countermeasures—once more, Russian countermeasures would likely hurt Russia more than Europe.

- Finally, the European Union and the United States could try to involve more third-party states into their campaign. This could be done cooperatively by diplomatic outreach, or coercively through the imposition of secondary sanctions to force third countries' governments and firms to choose between EU and U.S. markets and Russia. While such a move would hardly be a novelty for the United States, which has imposed such far-reaching measures against Iran, it would represent a new step for Europeans, who have long advocated against the legality of secondary sanctions. Still, nothing in the European treaties would legally prevent them from using sanctions more aggressively toward third-party states.

Sustain sanctions over time if the current situation doesn't change.

Sanctions can work only if the transatlantic community has the ability to sustain sanctions over time. As explained recently by U.S. Ambassador Dan Fried, the State Department coordinator for sanctions, "don't be in hurry with sanctions. If we maintain them, sanctions' impact will be felt more strongly over time. Russia sanctions have contributed to a weaker and stressed Russian economy." He added that "the Russia sanctions can buy time and space for Ukraine to implement the reforms it must implement to survive as a sovereign state."[43]

---

[42] Richard Nephew, "Issue Brief: Revisiting Oil Sanctions on Russia," Columbia University, July 2015, http://energypolicy.columbia.edu/sites/default/files/energy/Issue%20Brief_Revisiting%20Oil%20Sanctions%20on%20Russia_Nephew_July%202015.pdf.

[43] Ambassador Dan Fried, "Assessing U.S. Sanctions: Impact, Effectiveness, Consequences," Wilson Center, April 16, 2015, http://www.wilsoncenter.org/event/assessing-us-sanctions-impact-effectiveness-consequences.

Time is not going to play in favor of a Russian economy if it remains under Western sanctions. The data currently available in the April 2015 World Bank outlook of the Russian economy suggests several key lessons. Restrictions on access to equipment needed for the continued exploration and development of Russian hydrocarbon reserves could eventually degrade Russian energy production and reduce Russia's ability to export as much oil as it would like. Additionally, the decrease of foreign investments in Russia will further hamper long-term growth in a country that already suffers from an excessively low level of investment.

Finally, the difficulty in obtaining financing in the European Union and in the United States will slowly constrain the Russian financial market and lead Russian authorities to inject liquidities to stabilize it as necessary. This will further prevent required investment for economic growth, which Russia's poor demography will not boost anyway. Already, the IMF evaluates that sanctions could cost Russia up to 9 percent of its current real GDP in the next few years, although the institution did not indicate how many and cautioned about the potential uncertainties of model-based estimates.

Therefore, the transatlantic community needs to be able to sustain sanctions over time and to ensure Russia understands that sanctions will stay as long as necessary.

Sustaining economic sanctions against Russia. The European Union arrived at its decision to extend sanctions until January 2016 far more easily than expected because most of the larger European players agreed to it. It may become more difficult in the future if the cost of sanctions increases over time and turns significant players in Europe against sanctions. Solidarity mechanisms could make a useful contribution to render the cost of sanctions more bearable and sanctions themselves more acceptable. Within the European Union, for instance, European institutions were able to develop exceptional measures to support European exporters in the wake of Russia's countermeasures against European agri-food exports. The European Union provided this help through financial support to exporters and efforts to reorient exports to alternative customers. Europeans may consider extending such mechanisms to other sectors impacted by Western sanctions to help exporters and importers better cope with sanctions.

Ensuring Russia realizes that sanctions will remain in effect by lengthening the renewal period of European sanctions if they are renewed in January 2016. At that point, if the situation requires their renewal once again, European sanctions may gain credibility by becoming unlimited in time, in a similar way to the European sanctions against Iran, rather than time-bounded as they currently are. In other words, sanctions would be stronger if Europeans had to vote for their lifting, rather than to vote for their renewal every six months. Some countries within the European Union might fear that such legal reversal could be used by eastern member states to artificially maintain sanctions regardless of the evolution of the crisis in Ukraine, therefore turning them into sanctions about what Russia has become more than about what it is doing in Ukraine only. As a compromise, European sanctions could at least be renewed for longer periods of time—one year, for instance—a move that would not, in turn, prevent Europeans to lift sanctions earlier than that if the situation allowed it.

Ensuring Ukraine becomes successful. At the end of the day, sanctions will be useless if Ukraine cannot succeed as a stronger state and a more modern and liberal economy. In Ukraine, sanctions can therefore only be part of a broader strategy involving continued support and aid to the Ukrainian government to help it build a more resilient, less corrupt, and more developed country. The international community has supported Ukraine financially over the past year through the IMF and aid packages designed by the European Union and the United States. This should continue as much as possible as long as it can help current Ukrainian authorities push reforms and break endemic corruption. Ukrainians need to do their part, as it will be increasingly difficult for Europeans to continue paying the steep price of sanctions for a country that would not show itself to be up to the challenge. With Ukraine failing to do that, sanctions will become less sustainable because sanctioning countries will see such investment in Ukraine's future as pointless.

Although many Ukrainians may not agree with this assessment, Ukraine's short-term interests require it to halt hostilities against rebel groups and Russia, improve the security situation in the country, and focus all resources on building a stronger Ukraine, not necessarily to immediately restore sovereignty over its full territory. This must obviously remain a long-term objective for Kiev. But Ukraine is more likely to achieve this objective by becoming an attractive liberal and successful country— hopefully in a not-too-distant future—than by fighting for it today. Ukraine needs time—and financial help—and sanctions can buy that.

Russia, on the other hand, is likely betting that Ukraine will never "succeed" in becoming the reformed country and the emerging economy that can offer attractive prospects to its population. Entertaining hostilities in Ukraine is an efficient way to ensure it doesn't but also, when the time comes, to dictate to Kiev the terms under which Ukraine's eastern territories shall be reintegrated into its political system. Russia's best chance to retain influence in Ukraine isn't to annex eastern Ukraine, but to make sure separatists gain leverage on Kiev within Ukraine, not outside of it. Kiev, on the contrary, would be better off not rushing toward such reintegration, putting an end to hostilities for now and gaining strength to put itself in a stronger position to reintegrate eastern Ukraine on its own terms.

Ukraine and Russia's diverging objectives and strategies may put Europeans—and in turn, Americans—in a complex situation. If Ukraine actually intends to wait for reintegrating eastern territories on its own terms, it runs the risk of forcing Europeans and Americans to maintain sanctions for a longer period of time than may be necessary. Europeans are willing to see Ukraine being reunited sooner rather later, if Russia allows it on acceptable terms, considering the significant economic cost of sanctions. Europeans are therefore likely to put pressure on Ukraine, as well as on Russia, so that both parties comply with the Minsk II terms. Americans, for their part, do not bear the cost of sanctions and may therefore be more tolerant toward an

Ukrainian "delay" strategy. At the end of the day, all parties involved will need to tread very carefully. Ukraine must avoid creating frustration in Europe. The United States needs to take into account all European positions but also put sufficient pressure on Ukrainians. Such steps can help deprive Russia of an easy way out from a crisis it has created, for the most part.

Limit for now sanctioning Russia to its involvement in Ukraine.

Sanctions cannot address all issues arising with Russia beyond Ukraine. Sanctions should not be blamed for not doing things they cannot be expected to perform. Sanctions should therefore not be expected to address the broader challenge posed to NATO by Russia's new external assertiveness or deter initiatives Russia may want to take to test NATO's Article 5 in the alliance's eastern territory. Military reassurance and deterrence measures taken through NATO are more likely to be effective in tackling this potential threat. Likewise, reinforcing political, social, and economic resilience in eastern European countries will help them to deny Russia the potential benefits it may expect from a destabilization campaign launched against its European neighbors. Such an enterprise is most likely to be pursued through and with the help of the European Union in coordination with NATO when relevant or necessary.

Still, could sanctions play a role in addressing some of Russia's possible hybrid tactics? They might, in the context of a crisis involving Russian initiatives taking place on NATO's territory but not falling under the threshold of NATO's Article 5 and therefore being insufficient to trigger a military response by the alliance. NATO, as a military alliance, has no mechanism to introduce economic sanctions of its own—and it shall not acquire one. Any sanctions most likely would have to be implemented by NATO allies in a national capacity, or in conjunction with the European Union. These would then constitute a first signal of determination and could prevent an escalation into military activity, although given the direct threat to allied security, NATO member states could be willing to take military steps as well. To be more specific, one could envision sanctions to respond to destabilizing initiatives clearly attributable to Russia, created to spur social instability or cyber-attacks targeting sensitive infrastructure in one or more of the Baltic states.

But thinking about a role for sanctions in addressing Russia's potential hybrid tactics would not come without risks, as Russia could also interpret sanctions as a lack of determination to defend NATO's territory militarily. If the West responded to a security crisis on NATO territory initially through sanctions, Russia might misinterpret this as a lack of resolve. Such miscalculation would be dangerous for both sides as Russia may be more inclined to escalate if it does not expect a strong retaliation from NATO. NATO could then be convinced of the need to quickly move beyond sanctions and engage militarily.

Ultimately, the crisis in Ukraine is a symptom of a wider and structural evolution in the relationship between the transatlantic community and Russia. Sanctions have been useful to give the West leverage on Russia to contain its destabilizing policy in

Ukraine and eventually ensure a diplomatic settlement in Ukraine. Although unlikely in the near term, the crisis in Ukraine may be resolved and, in turn, enable the lifting of the sanctions imposed against Russia. This, in itself, would not get Russia's interactions with Europe and the United States back to what they were before Ukraine, as Russia's own domestic evolutions have largely complicated the cooperative spirit in which these relations were evolving in the post–Cold War environment.

Likewise, the lifting of sanctions imposed because of the crisis in Ukraine would not leave the transatlantic community unarmed—literally—to tackle Russia's challenges to Europe's security. Evolutions in military doctrines and postures, or negotiations with Moscow over the future of Europe's security architecture, are more likely than sanctions to achieve that in the long term. Full isolation from Russia isn't an option for Europe, if only for the simple reality of geography. Europe's future cohabitation with Russia remains to be defined, but the Ukraine crisis is a manifestation of a structural evolution in this relationship that will not simply go away, even with a full resolution of the Ukraine crisis. In that sense, lifting sanctions would not, and will not, mean returning to business as usual with Russia.

| Annex. Current State of European and U.S. Sanctions Adopted over Crisis in Ukraine

Transatlantic sanctions against Russia were adopted in five, mostly coordinated, rounds in Brussels and in the United States. An important difference is that European sanctions are time-limited, whereas American sanctions are not. European sanctions therefore need positive action to be renewed, whereas American sanctions need positive action to be lifted.

In addition to U.S. and EU sanctions, other countries imposed autonomous sanctions against Russia at the different stages of the crisis. Most of the time, those sanctions were closely aligned with, but not always exactly similar to, those adopted by the transatlantic alliance (mostly restrictions on arms and military trade and on Russia's access to financial markets). Those countries include Japan,[44] Canada,[45] Australia,[46] Norway,[47] Switzerland,[48] and obviously Ukraine[49] itself.

Early Individual Sanctions (March–July 2014)

The first round of sanctions was adopted on March 5–6, 2014, focusing on early individual measures adopted against persons identified as responsible for the misappropriation of state funds in Ukraine, and the freezing of assets of persons responsible for human rights violations.

- On March 5, 2014, the European Union adopted its Decision 2014/119, freezing funds and economic resources of persons responsible for the misappropriation of Ukrainian state funds and for human rights violations in Ukraine. Initially adopted for a year, this decision was prolonged for another year on March 6, 2015. These measures will now remain in force until March 6, 2016.

---

[44] Alexander Martin, "Japan Announces Fresh Russia Sanctions," *Wall Street Journal*, September 24, 2014, http://www.wsj.com/articles/japan-announces-new-russia-sanctions-1411553420.

[45] See Canada's Department of Foreign Affairs, Trade and Development website's section on "Canada Sanctions Related to Russia," http://www.international.gc.ca/sanctions/countries-pays/russia-russie.aspx?lang=eng.

[46] See Australia's Department of Foreign Affairs and Trade website's section on "Expanded Sanctions against Russia," http://dfat.gov.au/international-relations/security/sanctions/sanctions-regimes/Pages/russia.aspx.

[47] Saleha Mohsin, "Norway 'Ready to Act' as Putin Sanctions Spark Fallout Probe," *Bloomberg Business*, August 12, 2014, http://www.bloomberg.com/news/articles/2014-08-12/norway-ready-to-act-as-russian-sanctions-trigger-fallout-probe.

[48] Swiss Confederation, "Situation in Ukraine: Federal Council decides on further measures to prevent the circumvention of international sanctions," Press Release, August 28, 2014, https://www.news.admin.ch/message/index.html?lang=en&msg-id=54221.

[49] RFE/RL, "Ukraine passes Law on Russia Sanctions, Gas Pipelines," Radio Free Europe / Radio Liberty, September 14, 2015, http://www.rferl.org/content/ukraine-legislation-sanctions-russia/26530692.html.

- On March 6, 2014, President Obama signed Executive Order 13660 based on the finding that the situation in Ukraine constituted an "unusual and extraordinary threat to the national security and policy of the United States." The order authorized sanctions on individuals and entities responsible for violating the sovereignty and territorial integrity of Ukraine, or for stealing assets of the Ukrainian people.

The second round of sanctions, adopted on March 17, 2014, focused on further individual measures adopted against persons responsible for actions threatening Ukraine's territorial integrity, sovereignty, and independence (e.g., persons involved in the annexation of Crimea).

- On March 17, 2014, the European Union adopted Decision 2014/145 that put in place restrictions for admission, as well as freezing of funds and economic resources of individuals and entities compromising Ukraine's territorial integrity, sovereignty, and independence. Decision 2014/145 was initially adopted for six months, until September 17, 2014. It has been renewed three times since then, lastly on September 3. The decision is now valid until March 15, 2016.

- On March 17, 2014, President Obama signed Executive Order 13661, which expands the scope of the national emergency declared in Executive Order 13660 to the "actions and policies of the Government of the Russian Federation with respect to Ukraine." Although EO 13661 only authorizes sanctions (admission restrictions, blocking of assets, and limitations on resource transfers) on individuals and entities responsible for these actions and policies, it creates an important legal base for further economic sanctions against Russia.

Building off this legal basis, the United States adopted Executive Order 13662 shortly after EO 13661 on March 20, 2014. This new order further expands sanctions to persons operating in the "financial services, energy, metals and mining, engineering, and defense and related material" sectors of the Russian economy upon determination by the secretary of the treasury. It is under the authority of these two executive orders that the next rounds of American sanctions were implemented.

The third round of sanctions focuses on Crimea and on the ban by the European Union and the United States of certain transactions, such as investment or provision of sectorial services, with the region annexed by Russia.

- On June 23, 2014, the European Union adopted Decision 2014/386 enacting a first ban on imports of goods from Crimea and Sebastopol. This decision is amended and reinforced by another decision (Decision 2014/933) adopted on December 19, 2014, extending the ban to further transactions. The sanctions against Crimea were renewed in June for another year. They are now due to remain in force until June 23, 2016.

- On December 19, 2014, President Obama coordinated with the decision adopted on the same day by the European Union and signed Executive Order 13685, blocking "property of certain persons and prohibiting certain transactions with respect to the Crimea Region of Ukraine."

Sectorial Sanctions against Russia (July–September 2014)

The fourth and most significant round of economic sanctions against Russia was implemented in July 2014, following the intensification of the conflict in Donbass and the downing of flight MH17. These sanctions focus on restrictions targeting Russia's financial, energy, and military sectors. They were built on a creative structure combining the identification of sectors of the Russian economy with limited lists of entities belonging to those sectors and to which restrictions for trade and financing apply.

- On July 16, 2014, the U.S. secretary of the treasury issued two directives under Executive Order 13662 identifying Russia's financial and energy sectors as being open to American sanctions. The provision of new debt of longer than 90 days maturity or new equity is forbidden to entities identified in both sectors. The list of entities was further extended on July 30, 2014.[50]

- On July 31, 2014, the European Union adopted Decision 2014/512, putting in place several measures: an embargo on arms and related material, an embargo on dual-use goods and technology intended for military use or a military end-user, a ban on imports of arms and related material, controls on export of equipment for the oil industry, and a restriction on the issuance of and trade in certain bonds, equity, or similar financial instruments on a maturity greater than 90 days against identified persons in the Russian financial sector.[51]

A fifth and final round of economic sanctions was imposed early in September 2014 to intensify and extend the sectorial sanctions enacted in July.

- On September 8, 2014, the European Union modified Decision 2014/512, most notably to extend restrictions on the provision of debts and equities: the 90-day maturity limit for the provision created in July was lowered to 30 days for the same identified financial entities, and this restriction was extended to entities identified in the energy[52] and defense[53] sectors. The European Union also banned exports of goods, services, or technology in support of exploration or production for Russian deep-water, Arctic offshore, or shale projects.

---

[50] As of July 30, 2014, five financial institutions (Gazprombank, VEB, Bank of Moscow, Rosselkhozbank, and VTB Bank) and two energy companies (Novatek and Rosneft) were identified.
[51] Sberbank, VTB Bank, Gazprombank, Vnesheconombank (VEB), and Rosselkhozbank.
[52] Rosneft, Transneft, and Gazprom Neft.
[53] Opk Oboronprom, United Aircraft Corporation, Uralvagonzavod.

- On September 12, 2014, the U.S. secretary of the treasury issued four additional directives under Executive Order 13662.[54] The first directive tightened debt-financing restrictions by reducing the maturity period for new debt issued by financial institutions identified by the Treasury[55] from 90 days to 30 days. The second directive prohibited the provision of financing for new debt of greater than 90 days maturity issued by two additional Russian energy companies.[56] The third directive opened the defense and related material sector to American sanctions and prohibited the provision of new debt of greater than 30 days maturity to Rostec. Finally, the fourth directive imposed sanctions that, similar to the EU measures, target Russian deep-water, Arctic offshore, and shale projects.

European sectorial sanctions enacted by Decision 2014/512, including the modifications made in September 2014, have been initially adopted for one year. They were renewed in July 2015 and are now due to expire on January 31, 2016.

Finally, on July 30, 2015, the U.S. Treasury's Office of Foreign Assets Control (OFAC) announced an update of its Specially Designated Nationals (SDN) List with regard to the crisis in Ukraine—11 individuals and 15 entities were added to this list—and of its Sectoral Sanctions Identification (SSI) List—35 entities where added to that list.[57] This "maintenance" package was announced by the United States independently from the European Union and was "designed to counter attempts to circumvent our sanctions, to further align U.S. measures with those of our international partners, and to provide additional information to assist the private sector with sanctions compliance."[58]

---

[54] U.S. Department of Treasury, Office of Foreign Assets Control, "Sectorial Sanctions Identifications List," July 30, 2015, http://www.treasury.gov/ofac/downloads/ssi/ssi.pdf.
[55] On September 12, 2014, Sberbank was added to the five already identified in July.
[56] On September 12, 2014, Gazprom Neft and Transneft were added to the two already identified in July.
[57] For OFAC's recent actions, see U.S. Department of Treasury, Ukraine-related Designations, Sectoral Sanctions Identifications, July 30, 2015, http://www.treasury.gov/resource-center/sanctions/OFAC-Enforcement/Pages/20150730.aspx.
[58] U.S. Department of Treasury, "Treasury Sanctions Individuals and Entities Involved in Sanctions Evasion Related to Russia and Ukraine," Press Release, July 30, 2015, http://www.treasury.gov/press-center/press-releases/Pages/jl0133.aspx.

About the Author

Simond de Galbert is a visiting fellow with the Europe Program at CSIS and a French diplomat on detail. His primary research interests are European and transatlantic security, strategic affairs, and sanctions. Prior to joining CSIS, he served for several years in the French Ministry for Foreign Affairs, where he worked on Middle East nuclear nonproliferation and nuclear-related sanctions issues. He was an expert in the French negotiating team to the P5+1 nuclear talks with Iran from 2011 to 2014. He graduated from the French National School for Administration and Sciences Po Paris.